USBORNE

Unicorns
STICKER BOOK

Illustrated by Camilla Garofano
Designed by Mary Cartwright
Written by Fiona Watt

At the back of this book, you will find lots of stickers. Some of them are especially sparkly – can you find them?

Contents

2 In a forest
4 A secret garden
6 Swimming in waves
8 Ice castle
10 Magical cave
12 High in the sky

14 Starry night
16 In the mountains
18 Treetop nursery
20 Sunny meadow
22 Waterfall leap
24 A herd of unicorns
    Sticker pages

In a forest

Deep in a dark forest there's a secluded glade,
where unicorns gather to rest in the sunlight
that streams between branches of twisted trees.
Squirrels scamper playfully, while owls flutter in
to roost on the branches.

A secret garden

A cool stream babbles gently through a hidden garden, where unicorns meet to doze quietly in the shade of willow trees. Bluebirds soar through the air, as fish swim along the glistening stream.

Swimming in waves

As the sun sinks in the sky at the end of a sultry day, a herd of unicorns dive into the sea to cool down. They paddle and wallow in the waves, as shimmering fish glide and dart beneath them.

Ice castle

On a mountainside in the frozen lands of the North, lies a castle reached only by a gleaming bridge of ice. Unicorns trot gracefully across the bridge and roam the castle gardens, where icicles hang from branches and delicate snowberries grow.

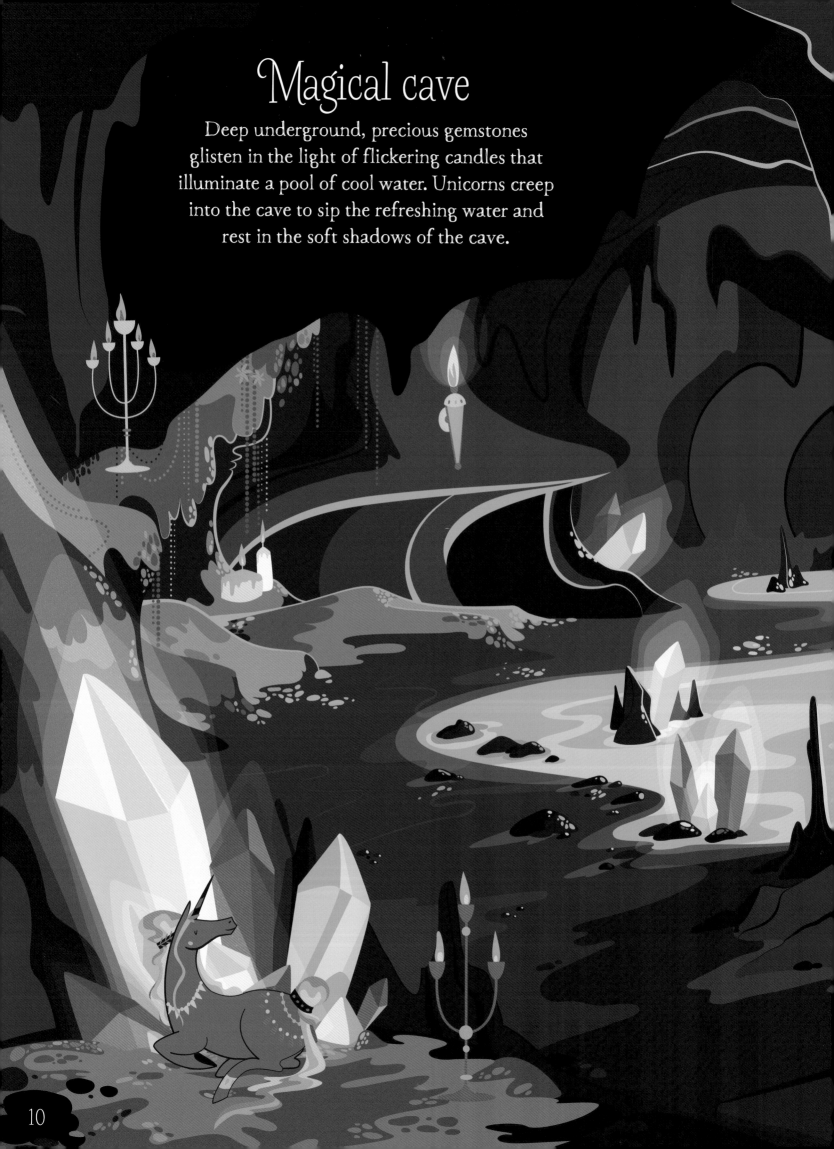

Magical cave

Deep underground, precious gemstones
glisten in the light of flickering candles that
illuminate a pool of cool water. Unicorns creep
into the cave to sip the refreshing water and
rest in the soft shadows of the cave.

High in the sky

High above billowing clouds, a rainbow
arcs across the sky. A flock of unicorns
stretch their rainbow wings and soar
gracefully through the air.

Starry night

Under the brightness of a shining full moon,
hundreds of stars sparkle in the dark sky
along with glowing fireflies. Sleepy unicorns
gradually fly in to rest in nests in the treetops.

In the mountains

A group of agile unicorns are leaping
between craggy mountaintops. They nibble
the tufts of grass and wild flowers that
thrive in the fresh mountain air.

Treetop nursery

Butterflies flutter and parrots screech in
the canopy of magnificent jungle trees.
Each year, unicorns flock to the treetops to
have their foals and take care of them until
they are old enough to fly.

Sunny meadow

Unicorns and their foals graze in a flower meadow among poppies, buttercups and cornflowers. Some rest beneath the shady branches of the apple trees, while rabbits take cover in the meadow's long grass.

Waterfall leap

Streams of water cascade down a magnificent waterfall, as unicorns plunge into the river below. They climb onto the surrounding rocks to dry their wings before leaping into the water again.

A herd of unicorns

Match the stickers from the last sticker page to the unicorns.
Look back in the book to spot where each one lives.

Juniper   Florenza   Marilla   Crystal

Amethyst   Amberglow   Moonflower

Sierra   Jacaranda   Cowslip   Asana

First published in 2017 by Usborne Publishing Ltd., 83-85 Saffron Hill, London, EC1N 8RT, England. www.usborne.com